THE SELF-CARE GUIDE
FOR
#THERESISTANCE

THE SELF-CARE GUIDE FOR #THERESISTANCE

A WORKBOOK FOR THE SOCIALLY-CONSCIOUS AND/OR STRESSED

SEEMA RAO

FIRST EDITION: 2017

LIBRARY OF CONGRESS CATALOGING-IN-PUBLICATION DATA
RAO, SEEMA
THE SELF-CARE BOOK FOR #THERESISTANCE: A WORKBOOK FOR THE
SOCIALLY CONSCIOUS/ SEEMA RAO—1st ED
P.CM.
ISBN 978-1545062197
I. SELF-HELP, CREATIVITY 2. EXPERIMENTAL LEARNING

ISBN 978-1545062197 ISBN 1545062196

14 13 12 11 10 / 10 9 8 7 6 5 4 3 2 1

CONTENTS

CARING FOR MYSELF IS NOT SELF-INDULGENCE, IT IS SELF-PRESERVATION, AND THAT IS AN ACT OF POLITICAL WARFARE.

AUDRE LORDE

HEY YOU,

IT'S BEEN TOUGH. WHAT ELSE HAVE YOU BEEN FEELING?

ITS BEEN

_____   ,   _____
      (feeling)   (feeling)

_____   ,   _____
      (feeling)   (feeling)

&   _____   .
        (feeling)

I'M WITH YOU.
SO, I'M SHARING THE TOOLS THAT I'VE BEEN USING TO KEEP MYSELF
FROM GOING BONKERS.

I HIOPE THAT YOU USE THIS SELF-CARE GUIDE TO KEEP YOURSELF
EMOTIONALLY FIT AND ABLE TO RESIST.

HELPFUL HINTS

KEEP THIS BOOK PRIVATE, SO THAT YOU CAN BE HONEST WITH YOURSELF.

USE THIS BOOK TO:

sketch

write

observe

discuss

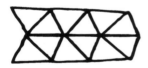

find patterns

make connections

make mistakes

try & try again

ON THE ORGANIZATION

THIS IS A HANDS-ON BOOK. YOU WILL NEED TO PUT THE WORK IN WORKBOOK. BUT, MAKE SPENDING TIME WITH THIS BOOK ENJOYABLE. DON'T JUST GRAB THAT RATTY BALLPOINT PEN THAT YOU FOUND. GRAB ANY AND ALL PENCILS, MARKERS, CRAYONS THAT YOU LOVE. IF NEED BE, GET SOME. THEY WIL GO TO GOOD USE.

THIS BOOK IS ORGANIZED INTO THREE MAIN SECTIONS:

PRIMAL WRITE
to get out the feelings--all the feelings

THE BEST YOU
to center yourself

ACT NOW
to help you hone your oppositional voice

YOU CAN GO THROUGH THE BOOK IN ORDER
OR DIP INTO SECTIONS AS THEY BECKON YOU.

IN EACH SECTION, ACTIVITIES THAT GO OVER MULTIPLE SPREADS ARE DENOTED BY GRAPHICS. TRY NOT TO SPLIT THOSE ACTIVITIES UP.

THE PATH OF THE BOOK

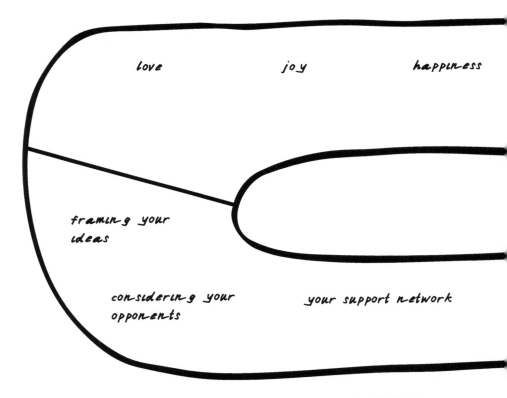

dealing with
negative emotions

thinking about
media use and
negativity

ACCLIMATE

love

joy

happiness

framing your
ideas

considering your
opponents

your support network

ACTION

APPROACH

looking for humor

mindfulness

ATTENTION

voting & actions

your mission
statement

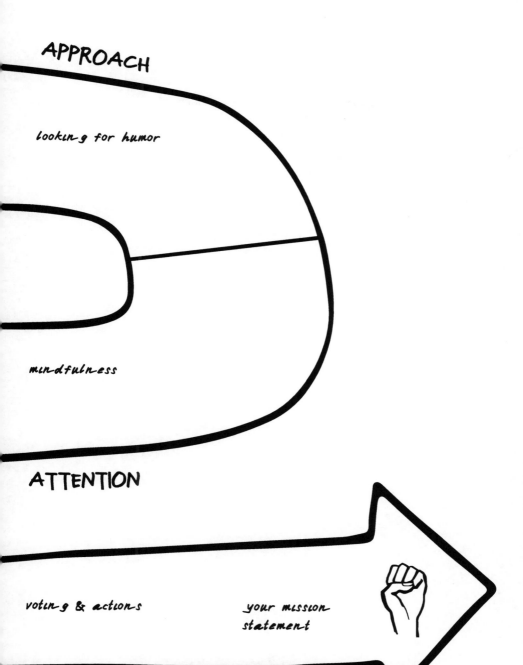

ANGER CANNOT BE DISHONEST.

MARCUS AURELIUS

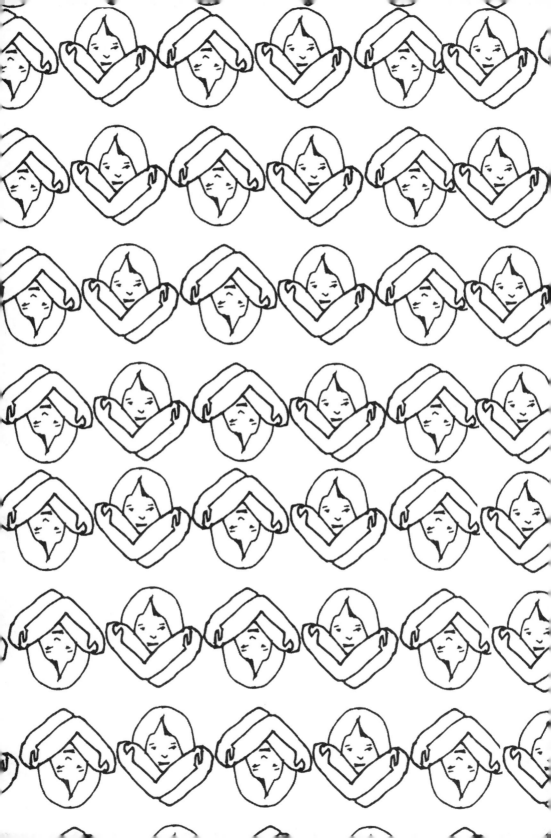

YOU PROBABLY HAVE VERY STRONG EMOTIONS. ALL THOSE
EMOTIONS CAN BE SCARY.

THIS SECTION WILL HELP YOU FACE ALL THOSE FEELINGS. STARTING WITH
NEGATIVE AND THEN TRANSITIONING INTO POSITIVE ONES. YOU WILL
ALSO RESEARCH THE EFFECTS OF THE MEDIA ON YOUR WELL-BEING.

DON'T SPEED THROUGH THIS SECTION. IF IT FEELS BAD, DO IT SLOWLY.
IF YOU ARE PARTICULARLY ANGRY OR STRESSED, FINISH THIS SECTION
BEFORE MOVING ON TO THE OTHER SECTIONS.

TAKE STOCK.

IT'S A GOOD IDEA TO START WITH ASSESSING WHAT YOU ARE
FEELING NOW. SORT YOUR FEELINGS BY COLOR.
grab some colored pencils, markers, crayons, whatever.

BLUE
very negative
feelings

GREEN
← between →
these

which colors dominate your page? any surprises?
any other observations?

YELLOW   ORANGE   RED
neutral feelings ⟵   between   ⟶   very positive
                          these   feelings

LET'S THINK ABOUT ANGER.

THE DARK CLOUDS OF ANGER CAN ROLL IN LIKE A STORM.
FILL THIS PAGE WITH ALL OF YOUR ANGRY FEELINGS.
COME BACK WHENEVER THESE FEELINGS COME BACK.

you might fill both these pages. you might not.

ANGER RARELY COMES ALONE. THIS EMOTION CAN BE TINGED WITH
OTHER FEELINGS. DRILL DOWN ON YOUR ANGRY FEELINGS.
WHEN SOMETHING MAKES YOU ANGRY, DOES IT ALSO MAKE YOU
SAD? CONFUSED? CATEGORIZE YOUR FEELINGS. *if you need more
categories, add them.*

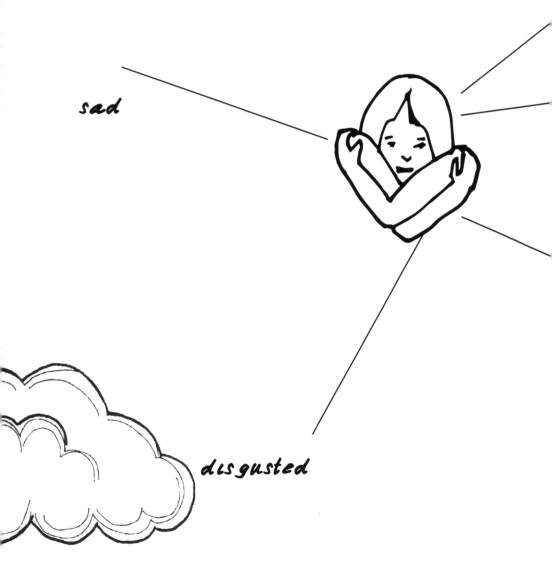

sad

disgusted

confused

scared

frustrated

FEAR CULTURE

ALONG WITH ANGER, FEAR CAN HOLD ONTO YOU. WHAT ARE THE THINGS YOU FEAR THE MOST? WRITE THOSE DOWN.

THEN, GRAB SOME COLORING TOOLS. TO TRANSFORM THOSE IDEAS INTO CONSTRUCTIVE ACTIONS. FOR EXAMPLE, IF YOU FEAR FAILURE, DRAW YOURSELF SUCCEEDING..

MEDIA FAST

NONE OF US LIVE IN A BUBBLE. THE NEGATIVE NOISE, ALTERNATIVE TRUTHS, NAME-CALLING . . . IT'S OUT THERE.. SOMETIMES YOU NEED A BREAK.

TRY TAKING A NEWS FAST.

FIRST, SET A GOAL.

I WILL FAST
FROM MEDIA FOR

DAYS

NEXT, SCHEDULE YOUR FAST IN YOUR CALENDAR. TELL YOUR FRIENDS YOU WILL BE AWAY FROM NEWS.

I WILL NOT CONSUME POLITICAL MEDIA

FROM   TO

BEFORE YOUR FAST, PLAN SOME DIVERSIONS. WHAT COULD YOU DO
INSTEAD OF CONSUMING MEDIA? WHAT THINGS ENGROSS YOU? HAVING
SOME STRATEGIES WILL SET YOU UP FOR SUCCESS.

WRITE YOUR LIST OF MEDIA FAST
COPING STRATEGIES

REFLECT ON YOUR MEDIA FAST.

WHAT HAPPENED?

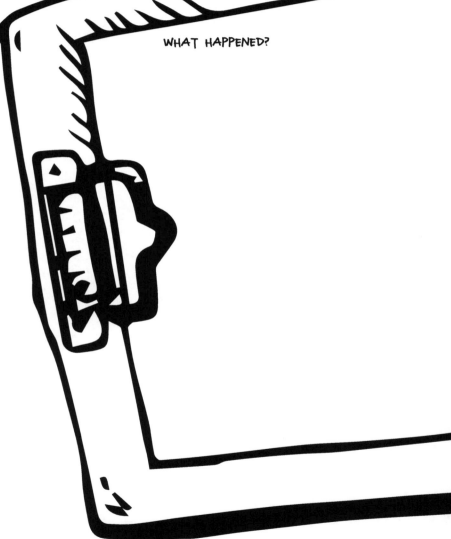

HOW DID YOUR MEDIA FAST
MAKE YOU FEEL? ARE THERE ANY
PATTERNS?

AFTER YOUR FAST, YOU NEED TO FIND A BALANCE.
#THERESISTANCE NEEDS TO BE INFORMED TO BE EFFECTIVE, LET'S
CREATE A REASONABLE PLAN FOR YOUR MEDIA DIET. SPEND ONE
DAY CATALOGING YOUR USE OF MEDIA & HOW YOU FEEL.
for each session, tally minutes of use & your feelings

NEWSPAPERS &
WEBSITES

FACEBOOK

TWITTER &
INSTAGRAM

FRIENDS &
FAMILY

YOU MIGHT NEED A LITTLE MORE SPACE TO CATALOG YOUR MEDIA USE.

NEWSPAPERS &
WEBSITES

FACEBOOK

TWITTER &
INSTAGRAM

FRIENDS &
FAMILY

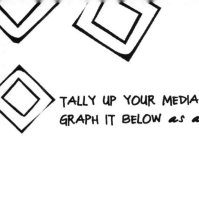

TALLY UP YOUR MEDIA DIET FOR YOUR DAY..
GRAPH IT BELOW *as a bar graph.*

HOURS

NEWSPAPERS &
WEBSITES

FACEBOOK

LOOK AT WHAT YOU SAID ABOUT YOUR FEELINGS.
FOR EACH BAR, ASSESS IF YOUR FEELINGS WERE ON THE WHOLE
NEGATIVE OR POSITIVE. *with blue for negative and red for
positive..*

TWITTER &
INSTAGRAM

FRIENDS &
FAMILY

WHERE ARE YOU SPENDING TIME THAT CAUSES
NEGATIVE FEELINGS?

WHERE ARE YOU SPENDING TIME THAT CREATES
POSITIVE FEELINGS?

PLAN YOUR IDEAL MEDIA DAY.

MORNING 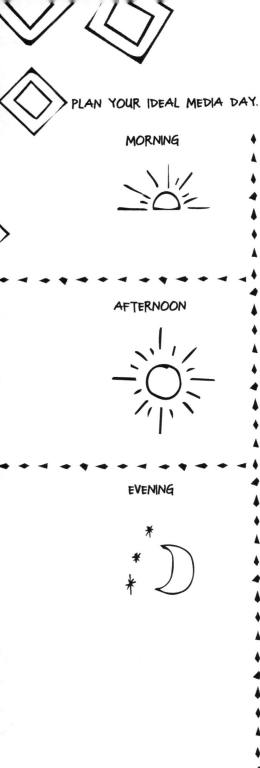   TYPE OF MEDIA

AFTERNOON

EVENING

AMOUNT OF TIME   REASON FOR USE

be gentle when you don't make this ideal.
just do your best.

SEEING THE HUMOR

WITH THE MEDIA MACHINE UNDER CONTROL, LET'S GIVE YOUR SYSTEM A SPIN.

HUMOR CAN BE A RESTORING EMOTION.

CARICATURE IS A COMICALLY EXAGGERATED DEPICTION.
IN TOUGH TIMES, ONE NEEDS A ROUGH LAUGH. LOOK FOR THE BEST EXAMPLES OF CARICATURE TO FILL THIS SPREAD...OR DRAW YOUR OWN.

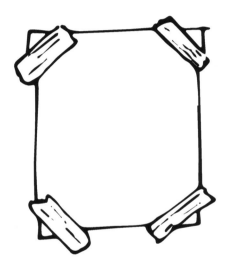

OPTIMISM IS THE FAITH THAT
LEADS TO ACHIEVEMENT.
NOTHING CAN BE DONE
WITHOUT HOPE AND
CONFIDENCE.

HELEN KELLER

THE

BEST

YOU

THE EXERCISES IN THIS SECTION HELP YOU MAINTAIN THE BEST YOU..

THE SECTION EXPLORES PHYSICAL WELL-BEING, MINDFULNESS, HAPPINESS, JOY, AND LOVE.

TAKE THIS AT A PACE THAT FEELS GOOD TO YOU. AFTER ALL, YOU ARE AT THE CENTER.

LET'S START WITH YOU.

DESCRIBE YOURSELF.

set the timer for 20 minutes. write all your best
characteristics. take a break. give yourself 10 more minutes
to write about yourself.

DRAW YOURSELF.
set the timer for 10 minutes. don't be scared. this is for you.
try not to judge yourself.

MAKE A PERSONAL TIMELINE .

EVERYTHING IS TEMPORARY. LET'S LOOK AT THIS MOMENT WITHIN THE SPAN OF YOUR LIFE.

WRITE KEY MILESTONES.. *mark your best moments.*
GO BEYOND TODAY, AND WRITE WHAT YOU HOPE FOR THE FUTURE..
add your future goals.

THE
BEST
YOU

MARK THIS MOMENT WITH A SMALL DOT. *this period is a blip in your life.*

TAKE CARE OF YOUR BODY.

 YOU CAN'T CONTROL POLITICS. BUT, YOU CAN CONTROL HOW YOU TREAT YOURSELF AND YOUR BODY.

BRAINSTORM WAYS YOU CAN ADD MORE MOVEMENT AND ACTIVITY INTO YOUR DAY. USE WORDS AND PICTURES..

KEEP A LOG OF HOW GOOD YOU ARE TO YOURSELF.

DAYS YOU EXERCISED LIKE
A BOSS

DAYS YOU ATE ALL YOUR
FRUIT & VEG

DAYS YOU DRANK
ENOUGH WATER

DAYS YOU MEDITATED OR
PRACTICED MINDFULNESS

THE BEST YOU

SINGING & DANCING COMBINE JOY & MOVEMENT.

MAKE A LISTS OF SONGS THAT
MAKE YOU WANT TO DANCE.
ASK FRIENDS FOR THEIRS.

PLAY THESE SONGS LOUD.
DANCE. DANCE. DANCE.

THE
BEST
YOU

KEEPING NEGATIVITY AT BAY IS HARD. YOU MIGHT FEEL NEGATIVITY OUT THERE LURKING IN YOUR RELATIONSHIPS.. YOU MIGHT FIND DARK FEELINGS WITHIN THE DEEPEST RECESSES OF YOUR MIND. PHYSICAL ACTIVITY, OF ANY KIND, CAN BE A CONSTRUCTIVE WAY TO COUNTERACT NEGATIVITY.

COME UP WITH SOME PHYSICAL ACTIVITIES TO DO WHEN NEGATIVE FEELINGS APPEAR. THE ACTIVITY CAN BE FAST OR SLOW. YOU CAN USE BIG MOVEMENT OR SMALL ACTION.

THIS CAN BE TOUCHING YOUR TOES EVERY TIME NEGATIVITY COMES KNOCKING. YOU COULD RUB YOUR TEMPLES, RUN AROUND THE BLOCK, FORCE A LAUGH, OR MASSAGE YOUR PALM....

THE ONLY CAVEAT IS THAT YOU SHOULD BE ABLE TO ACCOMPLISH YOUR ACTIVITIES ON THE SPOT WHEN NEGATIVE FEELING COMES IN.

YOUR LIST OF NEGATIVITY BUSTING ACTIONS

PREP YOUR MIND

GET YOURSELF INTO THE MINDSET TO TAKE CARE OF YOURSELF.
START BY CONTINUING THE LINE BELOW. AS YOU DO, YOUR MIND
WILL WANDER. KEEP BRINGING YOUR MIND BACK TO THE LINE.

WHEN YOUR MIND WAS WANDERING, WHERE DID IT GO?
(check all that apply.)

○ BOREDOM
○ ANGER
○ HAPPINESS
○ REVENGE
○ SADNESS
○ HUMOR
○ PEACE
○

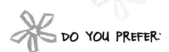 DO YOU PREFER:

SALTY   OR   SWEET

GRAB YOUR FAVORITE SALTY OR SWEET TREET TO EAT SLOWLY.
WHAT DO YOU NOTICE? WRITE ALL YOUR OBSERVATIONS AND
YOUR FEELINGS.

TAKE A WALK, BUT DON'T FORGET A PENCIL. WRITE AND/OR DRAW WHAT SURPRISES YOU.

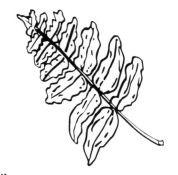

NOW, FIND SOMETHING NOISY THAT FEELS POLITICAL BUT POSITIVE. THIS COULD BE THE NEWS, A PROTEST, OR A TELEVISION SHOW..

CLOSE YOUR EYES. START DOODLING.

OPEN YOUR IDEAS, AND ADD SOME WORDS ABOUT YOUR FEELINGS.

YOU MIGHT NOT REALIZE THAT YOU ALREADY HAVE PRACTICES THAT CALM YOUR MIND IN A STRESSFUL TIME. EVERYONE NEEDS NEED AN ARSENAL OF CALMING TOOLS AT YOUR DISPOSAL IN POINTS OF EXTREME STRESS. HERE ARE SOME OF MINE:

TAKE 5 DEEP BREATHS

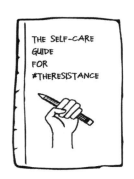

THE SELF-CARE
GUIDE
FOR
#THERESISTANCE

JOURNAL FOR 2 MINUTES

SIP WARM TEA

DRAW

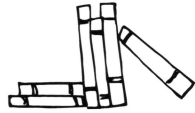

READ A BOOK

YOUR LIST OF CALMING ACTIVITIES

MINDFULNESS IS A LIFETIME PRACTICE. THESE EXERCISES ARE JUST THE BEGINNING. IF YOU FIND YOURSELF STRESSED OR SCATTERED, YOU CAN GO BACK TO THESE EXERCISES. YOU CAN ALSO RESEARCH OTHER MINDFUL PRACTICES. KEEP A LOG OF YOUR BEST MEDITATION TOOLS HERE.

THE
BEST
YOU

LET'S THINK A LITTLE ABOUT HAPPINESS.

THERE ARE THINGS THAT MAKE YOU SMILE. YOU CAN CALL THAT HAPPINESS.

THERE ARE THINGS THAT MAKE YOU FEEL LIKE YOUR HEART IS SMILING.. THAT WOULD DEFINITELY BE HAPPINESS..

TAKE TIME TO MAKE A REALLY LONG LIST OF ALL THAT MAKES YOU HAPPY.

dig deep.

come back later to add more.

TAKE ANOTHER PASS AT YOUR HAPPINESS LIST.
THIS TIME, DRAW THE THINGS THAT MAKE YOU HAPPY.

no one is judging your drawing.

TO MAKE HAPPINESS A PRIORITY, YOU NEED TO ANALYZE WHAT MAKES YOU HAPPY. MAKE A LIST OF THINGS THAT YOU DO THAT BRING YOU HAPPINESS. *hobbies, activities, exprienc es...*

REFLECT ON YOUR NOTES.

♡

mark the ones that you love.
DO THOSE MORE.

✖

mark the ones that feel hard..
KEEP DOING THOSE.

▬

mark the ones that feel unsatifying.
STOP DOING THOSE.

PLAN A JOY FEAST.

WHAT'S A JOY FEAST?

A JOY FEAST IS WHEN YOU PURPOSEFULLY, AND RARELY, OVERINDULGE IN THAT WHICH BRINGS YOU JOY. IT'S A PLANNED EXPERIENCE THAT MAKES YOU FEEL SPECIAL.

CERTAINLY A BIRTHDAY COULD BE A JOY FEAST, BUT SITTING IN YOUR JAMMIES BINGE-WATCHING YOUR FAVORITE SHOW COULD BRING YOU AS MUCH JOY.

A JOY FEAST COULD BE:

delicious

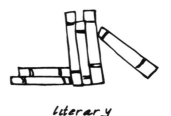

literary

creative

convivial

natural

individual

NOW, FOR YOUR JOY FEAST.

WHAT THINGS BRING YOU JOY? SKETCH THEM.

CIRCLE THE ONES THAT SEEM FEASIBLE. CROSS OUT THE ONES THAT ARE COST-, TIME-, OR HEALTH-PROHIBITIVE.

FROM THE ONES THAT ARE LEFT, PICK THE ONE THAT SCREAMS TO YOU.

NOW, PUT THE DATE ON YOUR CALENDAR.

MONTH 1

2 3 4 5 6 7
8 9 10 11 12 13
14 15 16 17 18 19
20 21 22 23 24 25
26 27 28 29 30 31

SCHEDULING IS A SIGN
OF COMMITMENT TO YOURSELF.
WHEN YOU DECIDE ON A DATE,
YOU ARE GIVING YOURSELF A
DEADLINE, AS WELL AS AN
END-POINT FOR YOUR PLANNING.
PLUS, YOU HAVE SOMETHING TO
LOOK FORWARD TO.

MY JOY PARTY WILL BE ON

_____

AT   TIME

_____

CREATE A LIST.

IN ORDER TO MAKE MY JOY
PARTY HAPPEN, I NEED:

DRAW YOUR PLANNED JOY FEAST.

annotate with your hopes and feelings

THE
BEST
YOU

I WILL INVITE:

○ ME   OR   ○ JUST ME

○
○
○
○
○
○
○
○
○
○
○
○
○
○
○
○
○
○
○
○
○
○

PUT YOUR EXPECTATIONS ON PAPER.

MY JOY FEAST WILL BE SUCCESSFUL IF:

I STILL NEED TO DO THESE THINGS TO
MAKE IT SUCCESSFUL:

DRAW HOW YOUR JOY FEAST TURNED OUT.

annotate with results and feelings

WHAT YOU HOLD DEAR

SOMETIMES YOU JUST NEED TO REMEMBER WHAT REALLY MATTERS. KEEP A RUNNING LIST OF ALL THAT YOU HOLD MOST DEAR. IN OTHER WORDS, CREATE A LIST OF WHAT YOU TRULY LOVE, WITH ALL YOUR HEART.

ACTION EXPRESSES PRIORITIES.

MAHATMA GANDHI

THIS SECTION IS ABOUT GETTING YOUR IDEAS TOGETHER FOR THE FIGHTS AHEAD. YOU WILL COMBINE FEELINGS AND FACTS INTO POWERFUL ARGUMENTS.

THE SECTION STARTS BY HELPING YOU HONE YOUR MOST IMPORTANT BELIEFS INTO COGENT ARGUMENTS. YOU WILL DO OPPOSITION RE-SEARCH AND HONE YOUR COUNTERARGUMENT. MOVING FROM YOU TO OTHERS, YOU WILL WORK ON IDENTIFYING YOUR SUPPPORT NETWORK. FINALLY, YOU END WHERE YOU STARTED--WITH YOU. YOU WILL DEVELOP YOUR PERSONAL MISSION STATEMENT.

ACT NOW

STEPPING BACK AND LOOKING FORWARD

DAYDREAMING ABOUT THE FUTURE IS OKAY, AS LONG AS YOU AREN"T DRAGGED INTO DARK, NEGATIVE THOUGHTS. USE YOUR POWER OF DAYDREAMING FOR GOOD. DRAW THE WORLD YOU ARE GOING TO CREATE.

WHY ARE YOU IN THIS? YOUR ARE IN THIS BECAUSE OF
YOUR CONVICTIONS. LET'S GET THEM OUT ON PAPER.

ACT NOW

99

PRIVILEGE

YOU CAN'T THINK ABOUT YOUR POLITICAL SELF WITHOUT ADDRESSING PRIVILEGE, BUT WE ARE ONLY TOUCHING ON THE TOPIC HERE. USE THIS BOOK AS THE BEGINNING OF YOUR EXPLORATION.

POWER IS PART OF SOCIETY. THE WAY YOU SEE THE WORLD IS DIFFERENT DEPENDING ON WHERE YOU STAND IN RELATIONSHIP TO POWER. PEOPLE BORN INTO GROUPS WITH GREATER POWER OFTEN HAVE CERTAIN ADVANTAGES OR PRIVILEGES. YOU MIGHT FEEL THAT YOU HAVE NOT PERSONALLY BENEFITED FROM BEING BORN INTO A CERTAIN CLASS OR RACE. THIS IS THE CHALLENGE WITH PRIVILEGE--IT IS HARD TO NOTICE UNLESS YOU DON"T HAVE IT.

PRIVILEGE CAN COME FROM BEING IN THE MAJORITY. IN AMERICA, WHITE PEOPLE ARE THE MAJORITY IN SOCIETY AND FAR OUTNUMBER OTHER RACES IN GOVERNMENT ROLES. THAT SAID, POWER IS NOT ALWAYS DERIVED FROM BEING IN THE MAJORITY. IN AMERICA, STATISTICALLY, THERE ARE MORE WOMEN THAN MEN, THOUGH MEN FAR OUTNUMBER WOMEN IN GOVERNMENT ROLES.

THIS EXERCISE IS NOT ABOUT MAKING YOU FEEL DEFENSIVE. INSTEAD, YOU SHOULD START TO FIND YOUR POSITION IN THE SPECTRUM OF PRIVILEGE.

REMEMBER, BEING UNCOMFORTABLE CAN MOVE YOU TOWARDS A PLACE WHERE YOU CAN MAKE THE WORLD MORE COMFORTABLE FOR EVERYONE.

THINK ABOUT THE FOLLOWING FACTORS. ARE YOU IN A GROUP THAT IS PRIVILEGED OR NOT? IF SOMEONE WERE TO DESCRIBE YOU, WOULD THEY USE A QUALIFYING WORD? *the difference between an artist and a woman artist or a doctor and a black doctor.*

RACE

GENDER

SEXUALITY

CLASS

EDUCATION

EMPLOYMENT

NATIVE LANGUAGE

PHYSICAL OR MENTAL ABILITY

AGE

WEIGHT

WITH PRIVILEGE COMES RESPONSIBILITY. LISTEN TO THOSE WITHOUT PRIVILEGE, HONOR THEIR FEELINGS, AND LEARN HOW YOU CAN ALLY YOURSELF WITH THEM.

ISSUE EXPLORATION

LET'S JUST SAY IT.
THERE'S A LOT WRONG IN THE WORLD.

AND, THERE'S ONLY ONE YOU. IT CAN BE OVERWHELMING. SO LETS
PRIORITIZE YOUR FIGHT.

the issues you are interested in

*pick one
of these two*

these are three to focus on

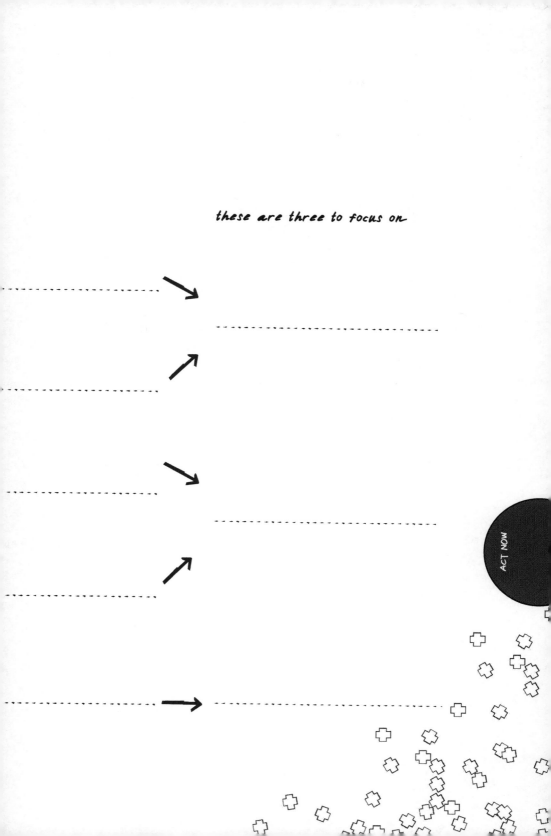

ACT NOW

PICK THE POLITICAL ISSUE THAT IS MOST IMPORTANT TO YOU FROM YOUR BIG THREE.

_____

WHY DOES IT MATTER?   WRITE ALL THE REASONS.

ACT NOW

NOW, REWRITE WHY THIS ISSUE MATTERS, BUT THIS TIME THINK ABOUT ALL THE PEOPLE IN SOCIETY CONNECTED TO THIS ISSUE. BE EXPANSIVE. DO RESEARCH. *(what does this mean for black women, gay men, disabled children? really work through this.)*

ACT NOW

NOW, MAP YOUR NOTES ABOUT THE ISSUE. MAKE SURE TO SHOW ALL THE PEOPLE & ALL THE CONNECTIONS.

{MY ISSUE:

THIS GRAPHIC BEGINS TO SHOW YOUR ISSUE CONSIDERED FROM AN INTERSECTIONAL PERSPECTIVE, where you see how your issue cconnects to people like you and people unlike you.

the fight is stronger when you realize its scope and breadth.

ACT NOW

BEING INFORMED WILL MAKE YOU BETTER AT RESISTING.

LET'S DO SOME OPPOSITION RESEARCH.

STATE YOUR ISSUE AS A BELIEF.

I BELIEVE THAT:

NOW STATE WHAT YOU PERCEIVE THAT THE OPPOSITION BELIEVES.

I THINK THAT THEY BELIEVE:

NOW CHECK THEM OUT.
FIND THREE SOURCES.. AVOID FAKE NEWS..
WHAT ARE THEY SAYING?

THEIIR POINT	SOURCE

ACT NOW

NOW FOR THE COUNTERATTACKS..
BEING ARMED AND PREPARED IS 1/2 THE BATTLE.
WRITE IN YOUR IDEAL RESPONSE TO THEIR ARGUMENTS. BE PITHY
THINK POSTER LOGOS OR TWITTER LENGTH. SHORT AND STRONG.
USE FACTS. USE REASON. USE TRUTH.

THEIR ARGUMENT

YOUR COUNTER ARGUMENT

ACT NOW

WRITE YOUR BEST COUNTERARGUMENTS LIKE YOU MEAN THEM. *write these words beautifully and with meaning.*

ACT NOW

YOU ALREADY HAVE YOUR COUNTERARGUMENTS. YOU UNDERSTAND YOUR CAUSE FROM MANY POINTS OF VIEW. YOU KNOW WHAT THEY WILL SAY. YOU KNOW HOW YOU WILL RESPOND.

so, grab your markers, colored pencils, or crayons and do it.

use this side to sketch out a few ideas or jot down some notes.

116

TURN THIS SIGN INTO YOUR BEST PROTEST SIGN..

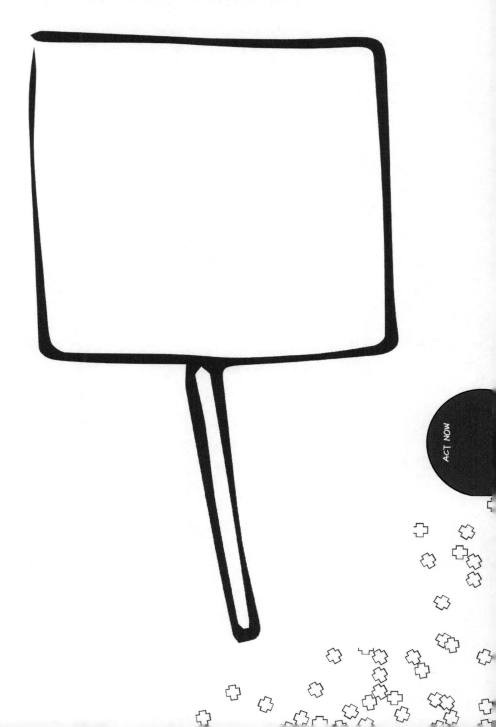

ACT NOW

YOU ARE NOT ALONE IN THIS FIGHT

TURN THIS SPREAD INTO YOUR IDEAL RALLY. FILL IN THE SIGNS.

ACT NOW

119

LET'S MAKE SURE YOU'VE GOT YOUR SUPPORT NETWORK.

WHO ARE THOSE PEOPLE WHO THINK LIKE YOU? WHO ARE THE PEOPLE
WHO MAKE YOU FEEL GOOD? KEEP THEM.

WHO ARE THOSE PEOPLE WHO MIGHT HAVE DIFFERING OPINIIONS THAN
YOU, BUT REMAIN RESPECTFUL, & HELP YOU STRETCH? KEEP THEM TOO.

LOOK FOR LOCAL ORGANIZATIONS THAT YOU CAN JOIN. DO YOUR
RESEARCH. ASK YOUR FRIENDS.

WRITE THE PROS AND CONS OF EACH PROSPECTIVE ORGANIZATION:

ORGANIZATION

pick the one that works best for you. contact them to join.

PROS

CONS

ACT NOW

VOTE! & AND KNOW YOUR LEADERS

ALL POLITICS IS LOCAL, SO THEY SAY. WHAT DISTRICT ARE YOU IN?

WRITE DOWN YOUR UPCOMING ELECTION DATES. MAKE SURE TO CHECK ON LOCAL ONES. DON'T MISS THOSE.

ELECTED REPRESENTATIVES:
LOOK UP WHO THEY ARE.. WHAT'S THEIR ADDRESS? EMAIL? PHONE?

CITY COUNCIL

MAYOR

STATE SENATOR

CONGRESSMAN

SENATOR

ACT NOW

LET'S GO BACK TO YOU

DESCRIBE YOURSELF AS AN ACTIVIST.
set the timer for 20 minutes. write all
your best characteristics when you work
on your cause. take a break.
give yourself 10 more minutes to write.

DRAW THE WAYS YOU HAVE ENGAGED.
set the timer for 10 minutes. don't be scared. this is for you.
try not to judge yourself.
take a break, and then give it another try.

THIS WHOLE SELF-CARE GUIDE IS REALLY JUST THE BEGINNING.. ONCE YOU BECOME OPEN TO PRIVILEGE AND INEQUITY THERE IS SO MUCH MORE TO KNOW. WHAT ELSE DO YOU NEED/ WANT TO EXPLORE?

ACT NOW

USE YOUR REFLECTIONS TO CREATE YOUR PERSONAL MISSION STATEMENT

A MISSION STATEMENT IS A SHORT PARAGRAPH. IDEALLY 2-4 SENTENCES, THAT SUMMARIZE WHAT AN ORGANIZATION IS ALL ABOUT. AN IDEAL MISSION STATEMENT ENCOMPASSES THE ORGANIZATION.'S GOALS, HOPES, AND REALITY.

IF MISSION STATEMENTS WORK FOR ORGANIZATIONS, THEY CAN WORK FOR YOU. START BY GOING THROUGH THIS JOURNAL. WHAT ARE SOME THEMES FROM ALL YOUR NOTES? WRITE THEM HERE.

CIRCLE THE THEMES THAT ARE MOST IMPORTANT TO YOU. THESE PHRASES WILL BE THE CENTER OF YOUR MISSION STATEMENT.

HOW DO THOSE PHRASES FIT TOGETHER? PLAY AROUND WITH WAYS TO STRING THEM TOGETHER IN A COUPLE SENTENCES THAT SUMMARIZE YOU.

ACT NOW

WRITE YOUR MISSION STATEMENT ON THIS PLAQUE. USE THIS SIDE IF YOU NEED TO MAKE MORE NOTES TO PREPARE YOUR IDEAL STATEMENT.

MY MISSION
STATEMENT

ACTION TALLY
YOU HAVE WORKED TO MAKE CHANGE. KEEP AN ONGOING TALLY TO
REMIND YOURSELF OF THIS.

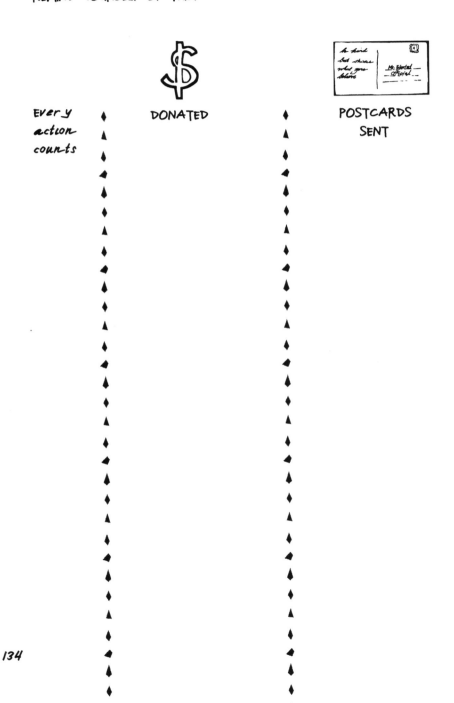

Every
action
counts

DONATED

POSTCARDS
SENT

CALLS
MADE

EMAILS
SENT

PROTESTS &
ACTIONS

ACT NOW

135

Every
action
counts

DONATED

POSTCARDS
SENT

CALLS
MADE

EMAILS
SENT

PROTESTS &
ACTIONS

ACT NOW

QUOTES

SOMETIMES YOU NEED A LITTLE EXTRA WISDOM. KEEP SOME EMPOWERING QUOTES HERE TO USE FOR INSPIRATION. WRITE THESE QUOTES WITH FEELING. *write these quotes beautifully to add to the pleasure of reading them.*

INDEX

INDEX

THANK YOU

THIS WAS A LABOR OF LOVE AND CATHARSIS. I WOULD LIKE TO THANK MY FAMILY, PARTICULARLY MY PARENTS, HUSBAND, AND CHILDREN FOR ALL THE SUPPORT THEY HAVE GIVEN ME OVER MY LIFE--AND FOR PICKING UP CHORES, AS I SCRIBBLED AWAY ON THIS ENDEAVOR. THANK YOU, AS WELL, TO NADINE KAVANAUGH, WHO IS AN AWESOME FRIEND AND PROOFREADER.

I WOULD ALSO LIKE TO THANK MY LOCAL LIBRARY FOR BEING A FREE RESOURCE FOR ALL THINGS FROM SELF-PUBLISHING TO HUMOR. IN MY MIND, LIBRARIES ARE THE GREATEST PUBLIC INSTITUTION OF OUR CIVILIZATION. LIBRARIES SERVE ANYONE FOR FREE. NO INSTITUTION IS MORE ACCESSIBLE. IF YOU DON'T BELIEVE ME, CHECK OUT YOUR LIBRARY. YOU WILL NOT BE DISAPPOINTED.

FINALLY, I WOULD LIKE TO THANK EVERYONE WHO ASPIRES TO MAKE THIS A WORLD IN WHICH ALL PEOPLE ARE TREATED WITH CARE AND KINDESS NO MATTER THEIR ORIGIN, GENDER, CLASS, RACE, AGE, APPEARANCE, AND/OR ABILITY.

ABOUT THE AUTHOR & ILLUSTRATOR

SEEMA RAO WAS BORN AND RAISED IN CLEVELAND, OHIO WHERE SHE CONTINUES TO RESIDE. SHE LOVES TO DRAW, EAT, AND READ. BUT, MOSTLY, SHE LOVES HANGING OUT WITH HER HUSBAND, YOUNG DAUGHTERS, AND INSANELY EASY-GOING DOG.

ACTIVE ON SOCIAL MEDIA, YOU CAN FIND HER AT:
HER BLOG: WWW.ARTPLAYSPACE.COM
INSTAGRAM: @ARTPLAYSPACE
TWITTER: @ARTPLAYSPACE

Made in the USA
Middletown, DE
24 December 2018